Looking at Countries

ITALY

Jillian Powell

W

FRANKLIN WATTS
LONDON•SYDNEY

First published in 2006 by
Franklin Watts
338 Euston Road
London NW1 3BH

Franklin Watts Australia
Hachette Children's Books
Level 17/207 Kent Street
Sydney NSW 2000

ISBN-10: 0 7496 6480 0
ISBN-13: 978 0 7496 6480 0
Dewey classification: 914.5

Series editor: Sarah Peutrill
Art director: Jonathan Hair
Design: Rita Storey
Cover design: Peter Scoulding
Picture research: Diana Morris

Picture credits: Age Fotostock/Superstock: front cover inset, 4, 11, 19, 20, 21b. Gaetano Barone/zefa/Corbis: 15. Paul Carr/Photographers Direct: 12. Bernd Ducke/Superbild/A1 pix: 25. Adam Eastland/Photographers Direct: 10. Kevin Galvin/European Stock Photo/Photographers Direct: 23. Dallas & John Heaton/Corbis: 27. Lumenstock/Corbis: 16. Stephanie Maze/Corbis: 22. Alberto Pizzoli/Sygma/Corbis: 26b. Olycom Spa/Rex Features: 24. Vinnie Streano/Corbis: 14b. Eberhard Streichan/zefa/Corbis:18. Superbild/A1 pix: front cover main, 1, 6, 7, 8, 17, 21t, 26c. Geray Sweeney/Corbis: 14t. Richard Wareham/Alamy: 13. Brenton West/Photographers Direct: 9. Every attempt has been made to clear copyright. Should there be any inadvertent omission please apply to the publisher for rectification.

A CIP catalogue record for this book is available from the British Library.

Printed in China

Contents

Where is Italy?

Italy is in southern Europe. It is a long country, shaped a bit like a boot. It is surrounded by five seas. The islands of Sicily, Sardinia and Capri are also part of Italy.

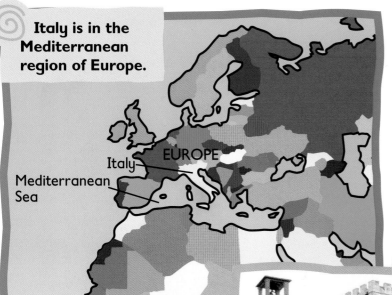

Italy is in the Mediterranean region of Europe.

EUROPE

Italy

Mediterranean Sea

Did you know?

Italians call Italy *Belpaese*, which means 'beautiful country'.

The Spanish steps are one of Rome's famous landmarks.

Rome is Italy's capital city. It has many famous buildings from the ancient Roman Empire. It also has smart shopping streets, sky-scraper offices and beautiful parks.

To the north, Italy shares borders with four other European countries. The high mountains of the Alps and the Dolomites lie on its borders with France, Slovenia, Switzerland and Austria.

Use this map to find the places mentioned in this book.

AUSTRIA

SWITZERLAND

FRANCE

SLOVENIA

CROATIA

Alps

Milan

Dolomites

Trieste

Venice

Turin

Genoa

Bologna

BOSNIA AND HERZEGOVINA

LIGURIA

LIGURIAN SEA

MONACO

Florence

TUSCANY

San Gimignano

Siena

ADRIATIC SEA

ITALY

Corsica

ROME

VATICAN CITY (Rome)

TYRRHENIAN SEA

Naples

Vesuvius

Capri

Pompeii

Positano

BASILICATA

APULIA

Sardinia

IONIAN SEA

Stromboli

Palermo

CALABRIA

MEDITERRANEAN SEA

Etna

Sicily

The landscape

Italy is famous for its beautiful landscape and coastline. The mountains of the Alps and the Dolomites in the north have snow-covered peaks, icy glaciers and fertile valleys. In their foothills are large and beautiful lakes such as Lake Garda and Lake Como.

Lake Garda is the largest lake in Italy and is a popular tourist destination.

Further south are huge areas of flat plains and rolling hills, crossed by rivers and streams. Grapes and olives grow here.

The landscape of Tuscany has many hills.

The landscape in the far south, and on Sardinia and Sicily, is rugged and mountainous. Italy has three volcanoes — Mount Vesuvius on the mainland, Mount Etna on Sicily, and the island volcano of Stromboli.

Did you know?

Mount Etna is the largest volcano in Europe.

Weather and seasons

Northern Italy is cooler and wetter than the south. There can be flooding after heavy rain in the autumn.

In the mountains, the summers are short and the winters are very cold with heavy snow. The highest peaks are snow-covered all through the year.

In northern Italy the first heavy snow falls can begin as early as October.

A strong wind called the Bora blows across the north-east in the winter months.

Did you know?

In Trieste, people put stones on house roofs to stop the Bora wind blowing tiles away.

Italy's warm climate attracts tourists to beaches like this one in Positano.

Further south, much of Italy enjoys a Mediterranean climate, with hot, dry summers, mild winters and some rain in the spring and autumn. In the far south, and on Sicily and Sardinia, it is generally hot and dry, and there can be long periods of drought in the summer.

Italian people

These women are dressed in folk costume for a festival in Rome.

Italy is made up of 20 different regions. Each has its own traditional food, folk costume, festivals and dialect. As well as Italian dialects, some Italians living in border regions speak French, German, Greek or Albanian.

Most Italians are Roman Catholics, although there are also Protestants, Jews and Muslims living in Italy. About a third of Italians go to Roman Catholic Mass regularly, and most celebrate important family and religious festivals by going to church.

A huge crowd in St Peter's Square in the Vatican City celebrates Sunday Mass.

In Rome, people gather to hear the Pope celebrate Sunday Mass in the Vatican.

School and family

These primary school children are wearing special smocks over their clothes while on a school trip.

Most children in Italy go to school between the ages of 6 and 15 years. Some children start earlier.

At some schools, lessons start at 8.30 am from Monday to Saturday and end at 1 pm. At others, school days are Monday to Friday from 8.30 am to 4.30 pm with a lunch break.

Family and home life are important to most Italians. Relatives often share childcare and enjoy going out and celebrating family events together.

Italians will take the whole family, including young children, when they are eating out – even when it is late in the evening.

Did you know?

Most women in Italy use both surnames when they are married.

Families enjoying the evening sun in a Venice square.

Country

The Italian countryside has many old villages and hill towns, which have changed little in hundreds of years. Here, some families carry on old ways of living. Many people keep a few pigs or chickens, for meat and eggs.

Italy's farmers grow crops such as potatoes, sugar beets, grains, grapes and olives. They also farm animals such as cows.

This man is harvesting olives in Tuscany.

Grapes have been growing in Italy since Roman times.

In this village in Apulia crafts, such as baskets, bags and pots, are for sale on the street.

Tourism provides jobs in many historic villages and towns. Local people work in hotels and cafés, or make craftwork, which they sell from their homes or at local markets. As there are fewer jobs in farming today, some village houses have become holiday homes for Italians or overseas tourists.

Did you know?

Bears and wolves live wild in the hills of Calabria, the 'toe' of Italy.

City

Scooters and trams can be seen on many of Italy's busy city streets.

Most people in Italy live in towns or cities, often in the suburbs, travelling into the centre to work. Apart from Naples, the main industrial cities are in the centre or north, such as Rome, Milan, Turin and Genoa. These busy cities have factories, banks, offices and shops. Milan is known worldwide for its designer fashion shops.

Millions of tourists from all over the world visit Italy's cities. The capital, Rome, has many famous buildings including St. Peter's Basilica and the Colosseum.

Venice and Florence are also popular cities for their beautiful buildings, churches, museums and art galleries.

Did you know?

Italy has over 3,000 museums.

Venice is built on islands in a lagoon and has canals instead of roads.

Italian homes

In towns and cities, and their suburbs, most Italians live in blocks of flats. Some are older blocks just a few storeys high; others are newly-built tower blocks. Most have balconies for sitting out.

People have hung their washing from some of the balconies of these flats.

🌀 **These houses in the hill town of San Gimignano in Tuscany are made with stone.**

Did you know?

In the Basilicata region in the south there is a 'cave city' of houses and churches built into the rock.

In the countryside, more people live in houses. Older houses are usually built from stone, with clay-tiled roofs.

Food

Italy is world famous for its good food and cooking. Each region is proud of its own foods and dishes, from salami from Bologna to candied ice cream from Sicily.

Pizza and pasta are popular foods from Italy. There are hundreds of types of pasta, and each region has its own pasta dishes and sauces.

Did you know?

Ice cream was invented in Italy over 200 years ago.

This man in Tuscany is making fresh pasta.

Bologna has a lively fish market.

Many Italians drink expresso coffee – a small cup of very strong coffee.

Although most Italians shop at supermarkets weekly, they also buy fresh foods from markets and small shops such as bakeries and butchers. Fresh local foods, for example tomatoes and olive oil, are used in many dishes.

At work

These women are making leather shoes in a factory near Milan.

In Italian towns and cities, people find work in offices, banks, shops and factories. There are many types of industry, especially in the north. Italian factories process foods, and make iron and steel, machinery, cars and clothes.

Tourism provides many jobs in hotels, restaurants and visitor attractions all over Italy. Nearly 40 million tourists visit Italy each year, for its food and climate, and to see its beautiful countryside, lakes and historic cities.

Did you know?

Italy is the fourth most visited country in the world.

This man is working as a waiter for an ice-cream café in Rome. Italy is world famous for its ice cream.

Having fun

Football, cycling, motor racing, basketball and skiing are all popular sports in Italy. Italians also enjoy the arts, such as opera, art shows and cinema. La Scala in Milan is the most famous opera house in the world.

Did you know?

Italy's football team are called the Azzurri, which means the light blues – the colour of their kit.

The Grand Prix is a world famous motor race held near Milan every year.

People dress up in costumes and masks for the Venice Carnival in February.

There are colourful festivals in all parts of Italy through the year. Some celebrate Christian festivals and saints' days. Other festivals celebrate the harvest of foods such as wheat or wild mushrooms. People dress up and there are often street parades or races. In Siena there is a famous horse race, called the Palio, through the streets in the summer.

Italy: the facts

- Italy is a republic. The president is the head of state and the prime minister leads the government. Italy is divided into 20 different regions. Five of them, including Sardinia and Sicily, have their own governments.

- Italy is a member of the European Union.

The Italian flag has bands of green, white and red.

Italians use the European currency, the euro.

The cathedral in Milan, Italy's second largest city.

• Over 58 million people live in Italy today.

• The largest cities are Rome, Milan, Naples and Turin. More than three million live in Rome.

Did you know?

Italians have around 16 public holidays every year.

Glossary

Basilica a large church.

Carnival a celebration in which people feast, hold parades and dress in costume.

Colosseum an open-air theatre built in Rome, between 70 and 80 CE. It was used for bloody battles between gladiators (fighters) for more than 300 years.

Dialect a local way of speaking a language.

Drought a long period without rain.

Fertile rich and productive.

Folk costume a style of clothes that has been passed down through generations.

Glaciers rivers of ice.

Grand Prix an important race of fast cars.

Head of state the main representative of a country; sometimes the leader of the government.

Lagoon a shallow area of water that is near or connected to a larger area of water.

Mainland the main land part of Italy.

Mass a Roman Catholic service in a church.

Mediterranean the areas that border the Mediterranean Sea.

Opera a musical play, in which all the words are sung rather than spoken.

Plains large areas of flat land.

Pope the leader of the Roman Catholic church, a branch of the Christian religion.

Republic a country with no king or queen, where decision-making power is held by the people and their representatives.

Roman Empire the lands ruled by the ancient city of Rome from 31 BCE to the 5th century CE.

Suburbs the area outside a town or city, where people mostly live rather than work.

Tourism work connected with holidaymakers and visitors.

Vatican a separate state within Rome, where the Pope lives.

Find out more

www.timeforkids.com/TFK/ hh/goplaces [Click Italy]
Information on Italy including a fact file, timeline, Italian phrases and quiz.

www.kidport.com/RefLib/ WorldGeography/Italy/ Italy.htm
A comprehensive guide including key facts, history and photos of Italy.

www2.lhric.org/pocantico/ italy/italy.htm
A website for children to learn about Italy including a short story and a quiz.

Note to parents and teachers: Every effort has been made by the Publishers to ensure that these websites are suitable for children, that they are of the highest educational value, and that they contain no inappropriate or offensive material. However, because of the nature of the Internet, it is impossible to guarantee that the contents of these sites will not be altered. We strongly advise that Internet access is supervised by a responsible adult.

Some Italian words

Italian word	English word	Say ...
arrivederci	goodbye	ah-ree-ve-der-chee
ciao	hello	chao
come sta?	how are you?	ko-me stah?
la famiglia	family	lah fah-meel-yah
grazie	thank you	grahts-ye
mi dispiace	sorry	mee dees-pyah-che
mi scusi	excuse me	mee sku-zee
no	no	no
per favore	please	per fah-vo-re
piazza	town square	pyaht-tsah
sì	yes	see

My map of Italy

Trace this map, colour it in and use the map on page 5 to write the names of all the places.

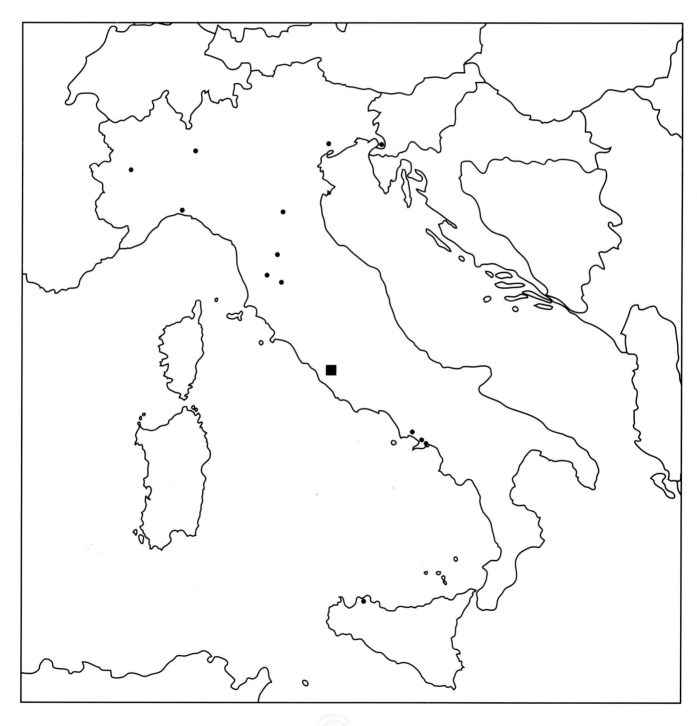

Index